GREAT GRACE

BILL VINCENT

GREAT GRACE

EMBRACING GOD'S FAVOR
IN SEASONS OF CHANGE

ArcanaVerse Books

CONTENTS

CONTENTS

TRUE APOSTOLIC LEADERSHIP

This book begins with a powerful assertion: the emergence of apostolic leaders, anointed for a new spiritual era. These devoted and wise prophets, ready to declare impending changes in leadership, signal a time for true apostolic power to unfold. As I started writing this sermon, a commanding voice from Heaven proclaimed, "True Apostolic Leadership is Coming." Months before, a prophetic message urged, "Apostles, come forth." Little did I know the demands this calling would place upon me.

"We must grasp the essence of apostolic ministry," I realized, "for it will soon envelop us." Samuel embodies this leadership, a man whose words never went unnoticed by God, nor did he depend on others for sustenance.

Samuel's life and ministry offer invaluable lessons for aspiring apostolic leaders, revealing key attributes God cherishes. A thorough examination of his life reveals secrets to becoming such leaders, aligning our hearts with God's in preparation. The Holy Spirit's descent upon Jesus, affirmed by a heavenly voice, parallels this.

Luke 3:22 describes this divine affirmation, as does the transfiguration witnessed by the disciples. These heavenly proclamations underscore a deep, established truth. Understanding apostolic leadership prepares us for its immense responsibility and power.

Samuel's intimate relationship with God ensured his words were never disregarded. 1 Samuel 3:19 highlights this unique bond, a model for us to speak only what is divinely revealed.

Galatians 1:12 echoes this sentiment, underscoring the necessity of divine revelation. Samuel's cautious approach to speaking in God's name allowed God to fully endorse his words.

Jesus, our ultimate example, demonstrated total submission to the Holy Spirit, speaking and acting solely on God's command (John 14:10). We, too, can achieve such alignment, ensuring our words align with divine will (Romans 8:14).

John 14:12 promises that those who believe in Jesus will perform even greater works, empowered by the Holy Spirit.

Samuel's integrity and humility, refusing to exploit his position, set a standard for future apostolic leaders (1 Samuel 12:2-4). Paul's admonitions to the Corinthian church highlight the importance of righteousness and wisdom in leadership, free from personal gain and grounded in Christ-like character.

The shared resources in the early church (Acts) demonstrate this principle of selfless service and unity.

Samuel, along with Moses and Aaron, exemplified leadership roles as intercessors and teachers (Psalms 99:6-7). Their faithfulness marked a pivotal shift for God's people, pointing towards the apostolic leadership of today. These leaders represent the merging of priestly, prophetic, and kingly anointings, crucial for transitional times.

The upcoming apostolic leaders will offer guidance and protection, akin to the cloud and fire that led Israel (Amos 3:7). Their roles will mirror those of Moses, Aaron, and Samuel, reflecting God's methods and intentions.

Understanding and revelation will be key in navigating these times, as the breath of God imparts wisdom.

Samuel's prophetic calling, despite his initial unfamiliarity with God, serves as an encouragement to those who may feel unqualified for such leadership (1 Samuel 3:7). Many modern-day leaders, akin to Samuel, might not have experienced the super-natural yet, but profound spiritual manifestations await them at the right time.

THE GLORY CLOUD IN MOTION

God is unveiling revelations like never before, and it's crucial that we move in sync with Him. I was immensely inspired when God confirmed His word through a vision. Directed to a specific chapter in the Bible, I found myself reading Numbers 10. This was unexpected, as my recent focus had been on Revelations, Daniel, Zechariah, and John's Gospel. Yet, this seemingly random passage resonated deeply with me, confirming the vision was divine.

In Numbers 10:1-2, God spoke to Moses about making two silver trumpets. This was not just a ritualistic directive but a profound call for Israel to gather and be ready to move with the divine presence. My vision translated a verse from this chapter as "increase, increase, increase, increase, increase," symbolizing God's desire for escalating blessings in the days ahead.

Numbers 10:28 speaks of the Israelites' journeying, which I interpret as a call for us to align with God's detailed guidance. This alignment is essential for us to experience His favor and grace, leading to progressive increase.

Isaiah 66:1-2 emphasizes the importance of humility, a contrite heart, and reverence for God's word in aligning ourselves with Him. These qualities are pivotal for the upcoming days.

The Lord instructed Moses in Numbers 10:14-16 to have three tribes - Judah, Issachar, and Zebulun - lead the procession. The lion emblem of Judah signifies the Lord's strength, reminding us of His resurrection power and victory. Understanding the times, as Issachar did, and acknowledging our heritage, as Zebulun represents, are essential for our spiritual advancement.

Deuteronomy 33:18-19 highlights Zebulun's blessing, transforming a region known for its darkness into a place of light and revelation, as seen in Matthew 4:15-16. This transformation is a prophetic symbol for places poised for divine encounters, especially along certain coastlines, though not exclusively.

The recent fall festival season was pivotal, marked by precise revelations about God's desire to not only demonstrate His Spirit but also enhance His presence among us. This is a time of significant spiritual harvest, and our role extends beyond evangelism to include mentoring and preparation for future harvesters. The divine presence is moving, and we are called to follow.

REALIZING GOD'S PURPOSES

We are at a pivotal moment in history where seeds sown over centuries are ready to bear fruit. It's a time to manifest all that God intends for us. Are you truly prepared for breakthroughs in your life, family, and ministry?

Isaiah 6:9-10 speaks of a people hearing but not understanding, seeing but not perceiving. This message, though seemingly discouraging, actually carries profound significance. It suggests that without spiritual awareness, people may miss their moment of divine visitation and the healing that accompanies it.

Matthew 13:11-16 expands on this, explaining why the mysteries of the kingdom of heaven are revealed to some but not to others. It emphasizes the importance of spiritual discernment and the consequences of its absence. These scriptures indicate that, had the people of that era recognized their spiritual visitation, they would have turned back to God and received healing.

Fortunately, the promise of scripture is that we don't have to remain blind and deaf to God's calling. Isaiah's prophecy may have been for a specific generation, but we are assured that the mysteries of the kingdom are accessible to us. It's our privilege and duty to seek the anointing of the spirit of revelation, illuminating our understanding to perceive the mysteries of the kingdom.

Ephesians 1:17-19 further emphasizes our right as believers to be endowed with the spirit of wisdom and revelation. This spiritual gift allows us to delve into God's heart, understanding His mysteries and our redeemed rights. It's not just intellectual wisdom but a divine impartation enabling us to perceive Jesus Christ and comprehend His plans and purposes.

This wisdom reveals the profound secrets of God hidden in Christ, fostering deeper intimacy with Him and a more profound understanding of divine truths. The accompanying spirit of revelation helps us comprehend these mysteries, applying them practically in our lives. The Apostle Paul exemplified this spirit, unveiling kingdom mysteries to his contemporaries. Similarly, we are called to discern the secrets reserved for the end times.

Daniel 12:4 prophesies a time when knowledge will increase, a period we are entering. Ephesians 1:18-19 outlines three blessings crucial for walking in Christ's full measure: understanding the hope of His calling, the riches of His inheritance in the saints, and the greatness of His power toward believers. While these promises are intellectually acknowledged, they are experientially realized through the spirit of wisdom and revelation.

We are granted the opportunity to fully embrace this profound mystery. In this era, we are anointed to understand and experience these mysteries through the power of redemption. Among these mysteries is the concept of "Christ in us, the hope of glory." While often spoken, its full reality is yet to be experienced by many.

However, scripture promises that a body of believers will soon emerge, fully embodying this truth, demonstrating Christ's power, authority, and nature. Notably, the full revelation of this mystery requires the merging of worship and prophecy, as illustrated when Elisha discerned God's voice more clearly with the minstrel's music. This partnership between worship and prophecy is becoming more pronounced, shaping services where worship continues seamlessly with the prophetic word.

EMBRACING THE RESTORATION
OF THE SOUL

Often, the most significant breakthroughs we need occur within our souls. I have personally experienced God's restoration of my soul, especially during a challenging time when my ministry team turned their backs on me following a controversial decision I made. This experience taught me that God's love and restoration are ever-present.

Job 33:29-30 speaks of God working to bring our souls back from despair, enlightening us with the light of life. Psalms 23:3 echoes this sentiment, emphasizing God's role in restoring our souls and guiding us towards righteousness.

The Apostle Paul, inspired by the Holy Spirit, prayed for the Thessalonians that God would sanctify their spirit, soul, and body (1 Thessalonians 5:23). This highlights the comprehensive nature of redemption, which aims to sanctify not just our spirit but also our soul and body. God's focus on the soul reflects His desire for complete dominion in all aspects of our lives, fostering un-impeded communion with Him. The soul, comprising our mind, will, and emotions, is where our feelings, desires, and affections reside.

Galatians 5:19-21 lists the works of the flesh, contrasting them with the fruits of the Spirit. When the temple veil was torn, it symbolized the removal of barriers between us and God. Similarly, any veils over our souls need to be removed through the 'water of the word' for sanctification.

Psalms 18:28 and Hebrews 4:12 convey that God's word is a light in our darkness and sharper than any two-edged sword, piercing to the division of soul and spirit. This word reveals and sanctifies the deepest parts of our being.

Abraham's story illustrates this purification process of the soul for complete unity with God. His love for Isaac, though profound, became a test of his soul's devotion to God. Abraham's willingness to sacrifice Isaac demonstrated his complete dedication, allowing him to experience a deeper level of worship.

Galatians 2:20 encapsulates the Christian's identification with Christ's death and life. Alexander Dowie's story serves as a cautionary tale about the dangers of spiritual deception. Despite his significant contributions to the ministry of healing, he was misled by a false prophecy, illustrating the need for continual spiritual vigilance and purity.

John 14:30 highlights that there was no place in Jesus for Satan's corruption. Similarly, we should strive for such spiritual integrity, ensuring no aspect of our carnal nature is susceptible to temptation.

This chapter calls us to introspection and purification of our souls, encouraging us to seek the Holy Spirit's guidance in identifying and relinquishing carnal tendencies. Embracing this process opens the door to perfect fellowship with God.

2 Peter 1:3-4 offers a glorious promise: God has given us everything needed for life and godliness through His divine power. By embracing His promises, we can partake in the divine nature and

escape worldly corruption. This path of restoration offers us rest for our souls, aligning us more closely with God's nature and will.

NAVIGATING TRANSITION

Transition is not just a concept; it's a dynamic process. It signifies God's movement in our lives, leading us from the old into the new. My extensive teaching on this subject aims to provide guidance for those undergoing such changes. This chapter will uncover a key element for navigating transitions successfully: the significance of consecration, staying in the Secret Place, and understanding why sanctification is crucial for the manifestation of God's wonders on Earth. You'll learn how your closeness with God impacts not only your life but also the nations.

Hebrews 13:5 and Psalms 119:105 remind us of God's constant presence and guidance, especially during uncertain times. Transition implies moving towards a specific destination, and to avoid aimless wandering, God offers a "spiritual compass" pointing directly to the Father's heart, found in the Secret Place. This chapter focuses on establishing spiritual stability during transitions by exploring key concepts like consecration and the benefits of sanctification, beginning with Leviticus 8:33-35.

The number seven symbolizes completion and perfection in the Bible. The seven days of consecration for Aaron and his sons were crucial for preparing them for their priestly roles. The eighth day, symbolizing new beginnings, was marked by God's appearance and the manifestation of His glory.

This process of consecration, akin to suffering, is essential for purification and the eventual revelation of God's glory, as emphasized in Romans 8:17-18. Embracing God's dealings now, rather than facing judgment later, is a wise choice. The story of Aaron's sons (Leviticus 10:1-2) serves as a cautionary tale about the consequences of deviating from God's presence.

The importance of remaining in God's presence is exemplified by Joshua, who led the Israelites into the Promised Land. His unwavering dedication to the tabernacle positioned him for God's anointing and leadership (Exodus 33:11). Similarly, our spiritual vitality depends on our commitment to the Secret Place.

Joshua's instruction to the people in Joshua 3:5 emphasizes the importance of sanctification in witnessing God's wonders. Sanctification sets us apart for God's purposes, as Moses' life illustrates. God's promise to Moses in Exodus 34:10 was made in the context of a covenant for holy living.

Exodus 33:1-3 highlights God's promise to Moses about the inheritance of the Promised Land. Yet, Moses desired more than the fulfillment of promises; he sought God's presence, the most crucial element for the journey (Exodus 33:14, 17).

This chapter emphasizes the power of intimacy with God in intercession, as demonstrated by Moses' history with the Lord. Leviticus 10:7 shows the significance of remaining steadfast in God's presence. Those who embrace this calling of intimacy and intercession, like Moses, can influence divine outcomes and carry the mantle of priestly ministry.

This chapter underscores the importance of sanctification, consecration, and remaining in the Secret Place during transitions.

These spiritual disciplines not only guide us through changes but also enable us to experience God's glory and favor, setting us apart for His purposes. As we navigate transitions, our focus should be on deepening our relationship with God, ensuring His presence remains central in our journey.

Exodus 33:16 poignantly asks how it can be known that God's grace is with us, and answers that it's through His presence that we are set apart. For those navigating transitions, this time is an opportunity to deepen your intercession, drawing on your history with God. Like Moses, your prayers can have a global impact, whether for your nation or others. This is a vital role in these challenging times.

Upon receiving God's favor, Moses immediately sought a deeper understanding of God's nature (Exodus 33:17-18). God's response in Exodus 33:19 reveals that His glory manifests through His goodness. This is a profound revelation for believers: experiencing God's goodness is an intimate encounter with His glory.

Moses was instructed to stand upon a rock, a symbol of being hidden in Christ (Exodus 33:21-22). In this season, embracing hiddenness in the 'cleft of the rock' is crucial. It's in this spiritual posture of humility that we can receive God's goodness.

Exodus 34:5 and 10 depict a divine visitation and covenant with God, promising marvels unprecedented in history. This promise of divine works and wonders is linked to our willingness to embrace a season of hiddenness.

When Moses descended Mount Sinai, his face shone with God's glory, yet he was unaware of it (Exodus 34:29). This teaches us a vital lesson: the greater glory comes when we lose sight of ourselves and become completely absorbed in serving God.

We yearn for a revival marked by power and resurrection, but this requires a deep commitment to God's presence. Like Joshua, we must seek the inner reality of the Lord. God's visitation will bring the wonders we desire and need, distinguishing us from all other nations and beliefs.

However, this journey starts with self-emptying. Let the Holy Spirit guide you during this transition, leading you to the tabernacle, the secret place of God's presence. Here, you will gain understanding and revelation, experience restoration, and be anointed for breakthrough and victory. In this sacred space, you'll find the strength and guidance to navigate your transition, emerging with a renewed sense of purpose and divine direction.

THE POWER OF PROPHETIC DECREES

This chapter emerges from a teaching series that I have yet to complete, despite preaching on it for over three hours. Here, I aim to help you comprehend the purpose behind God's prophetic words, visions, and revelations. We'll explore the obstacles that hinder the fulfillment of these divine messages in our lives and learn how to actively engage with them for successful realization.

Many believers have prophetic words spoken over their lives, yet they remain unfulfilled. We often find ourselves missing the mark of our calling. This chapter will delve into understanding and appropriating what God has promised. We'll explore strategies for warring for our prophetic words and how to effectively engage in spiritual warfare to bring these promises to fruition.

2 Peter 1:19 highlights the importance of heeding prophecy as a light shining in dark places. Yet, many of us are still waiting for the realization of prophetic words, wondering how to activate them in our lives. Is the delay due to the prophet, ourselves, or

spiritual opposition? Often, it's a mix of all these factors, including our own inaction or misalignment with God's potential for us.

There is an eternal dimension to God's promises, existing even before the creation of the world. These promises are available in the spiritual realm, waiting to be manifested in the natural. Our role is to perceive these promises through faith, embrace them, and declare them into existence.

Prophetic decrees have the power to transform our lives. They can counteract the plans of the enemy and expedite the fulfillment of God's words over us. When I learned to make prophetic decrees, I witnessed rapid advancements in my spiritual life. The Lord revealed that these decrees also dispatch angels to battle against forces opposing our divine inheritance.

In Matthew 16:13-16, Jesus asks His disciples about His identity. Peter's revelation that Jesus is the Christ is a divine inspiration from the Father. Similarly, you might have received a divine word or vision. These prophetic promises are specific and in alignment with God's Word. They hold the potential to activate our divine destiny.

Matthew 16:18 speaks of building the church upon the rock of revelation – understanding and acting upon divine inspiration. Jeremiah 24:6 and 42:10 reinforce this idea, indicating that God's revelations are meant to build and plant us in our divine purpose.

Matthew 16:19 talks about the keys of the kingdom – every prophetic word and revelation we receive. These keys unlock our destinies and enable us to bring heavenly realities to earth. However, many of us carry unused keys, forgetting their purpose and power.

It's essential to understand how to use these keys. Jesus' message to Peter about revelation shows us that we have a responsibility to unlock and manifest these divine insights. When God reveals something, it's often for immediate action, not distant future.

Delays in realizing prophetic words often arise from our lack of response, not just from spiritual opposition or divine timing. When God speaks a word over us, it is an invitation to change our identity and align with His vision.

The fulfillment of prophecy is conditional on our response and obedience. We may reach heaven only to realize the vast potential we never tapped into on earth. Consider Daniel, who, upon understanding Jeremiah's prophecy (Daniel 9:2), didn't just acknowledge it; he actively engaged in prayer and fasting to bring it to fruition.

Remember, there is often spiritual opposition to prophetic fulfillment. Daniel's experience shows us that delays can occur in the spiritual realm, not because the word is untrue, but due to resistance from the enemy.

The enemy's strategy is to thwart God's plans at their inception. He aims to discourage believers right at their moments of breakthrough. Understanding this, we must persist in faith and action to see God's promises come to pass.

In Genesis 50:24, Joseph assures his brethren of God's promise to lead them to a land sworn to their forefathers. This theme of divine promise and deliverance is echoed in the stories of Moses and Jesus, where attempts were made to thwart God's plans right at their infancy. In both instances, as in Exodus 2 and Matthew 2:16, we see a pattern of opposition to God's ordained purpose.

Satan's strategy has always been to undermine God's plan, whether it was Moses, Jesus, or us today. He tirelessly works to distract, delay, and destroy the fulfillment of our divine promises. His schemes include assigning spiritual adversaries to prevent us from discerning and fulfilling God's will.

Philippians 3:14 reminds us to press on despite these challenges, aiming for the high calling of God in Christ Jesus. The enemy may try to entrap us in various ways, but our destiny unfolds as we respond positively to God's promises. While God's covenants, like those with Israel and through Christ, remain unchangeable, He adjusts His responses based on our actions. Instances like Abraham's intercession for Sodom and Gomorrah, or Jonah's prophecy to Nineveh, show God's responsiveness to human repentance and intercession.

God's prophetic words are not just inevitable outcomes; they require our active participation. Like Jonah, we have a role in the fulfillment of these prophecies. Our response, or lack thereof, can significantly influence the course of events prophesied.

Our spiritual journey involves recognizing and combating the spiritual forces against us, as described in Ephesians 6:12. We must be spiritually vigilant, understanding that there's a constant battle over our destiny.

Mary's response to the angelic announcement in Luke 1:38 exemplifies aligning oneself with God's word. By agreeing with the heavenly message, she actively participated in bringing the prophecy to fruition.

Proverbs 8:15 and Romans 5:17 affirm our authority as spiritual kings, called to declare God's will on earth. Our declarations have the power to manifest God's promises in our lives and our world.

The revelation John received in Revelation 19:11-16 symbolizes the power of God's word as a weapon in spiritual warfare. Similarly, we must wield the prophetic words given to us, judiciously engaging in spiritual battles to see God's promises realized.

Acts 13:2 illustrates the Holy Spirit's guidance in fulfilling God's call. When God reveals His plans, it is our responsibility to embrace and intercede for their realization.

Understanding the spiritual dynamics at play, we can confidently approach God, trusting in His promises and our authority in Christ to manifest them. Everything we need for our calling is available in the spiritual realm, waiting to be claimed and brought into the physical world.

Mark 11:24 underscores the principle of faith in prayer: believing in receiving what we pray for. This concept is pivotal in understanding how we can make spiritual withdrawals from God's resources to fulfill our calling. It's not about idly waiting for blessings to fall from heaven; it involves active engagement through fasting, praying, and making prophetic decrees.

Prophetic decrees play a crucial role in the kingdom of God. They can dismantle the enemy's works and infuse life into God's people. However, words spoken carelessly or negatively, as highlighted in Psalm 64:1-4, can cause significant harm. King David equates our words to arrows, capable of wounding others, including ourselves. Our speech can either build or destroy, as Proverbs 18:21 warns.

The power of our words extends to speaking life, healing, and blessing. We're encouraged to speak positively about others and declare what God says about them and us. Prophetic decrees, aligned with God's promises in Scripture or revealed through prophecy, have the power to manifest these promises.

When we receive a word from God, it's our responsibility to seize it with faith. We're called to vocalize God's promises, enforcing them in heaven and on earth. Our mouths are the bows; the arrows are the Lord's words, used by God to deliver us from adversity.

Understanding the authority behind our decrees is crucial. Decrees, whether in the natural or spiritual realm, carry significant weight. They are like legal commands, enforceable and authoritative. In the Bible, decrees made by kings were respected and feared. If earthly decrees hold such power, imagine the force behind spiritual decrees made by believers, whom Scripture refers to as priests and kings (1 Peter 2:5; Revelation 1:4-6).

As divinely appointed priests and kings, our decrees in the spiritual realm have immense power. They are backed by the authority of heaven and Jesus Christ. When we speak in alignment with God's will, angels act to fulfill His word in our lives.

This is spiritual warfare. The enemy is aware of our uncertainty in our authority. To counter this, we must seek a deeper understanding of our identity in Christ. Scriptures like John 1:12, Romans 5:1, and Ephesians 2:10 provide assurance of our position in Him.

Are you ready to make prophetic decrees? Picture the scene in "Brave Heart," where archers release their fiery arrows in unison. Similarly, as we decree God's promises, the spiritual realm responds.

Begin by proclaiming God's promises over your life. Speak against any opposing forces and declare God's will for revival, miracles, health, and salvation. Use your authority to counteract the enemy's plans.

Remember, spiritual aggression is key in contending for our destiny. Matthew 11:12 speaks of the violent taking the kingdom by force, indicating the need for proactive spiritual pursuit. We must be zealous and earnest in laying hold of what God has promised.

In conclusion, your prophetic decrees have the potential to bring heaven's promises to earth. Speak life, declare healing, and claim victory over every area of your life. Be bold and relentless in your spiritual warfare, using your words as arrows to claim what God has decreed for you.

CULTIVATING A VICTORIOUS LIFE

This chapter is dedicated to inspiring you to live a life of victory every day. We will explore how our words, thoughts, associations, giving, and experiencing God's favor can significantly impact our spiritual growth. By adopting a gentle and uplifting approach to these five essential aspects, you will deepen your relationship with the Lord and learn how He desires for you to flourish physically, financially, emotionally, and spiritually.

Expect to witness signs, wonders, and breakthroughs as you embrace and implement these principles in your walk with Christ.

Mark 10:29-30 emphasizes that sacrifices made for Christ and the Gospel will be rewarded both now and in eternity. Similarly, 3 John 1:2 reflects God's wish for our prosperity and well-being in every aspect of life. As we trust in Him, we will experience His faithfulness and blessings.

Psalms 84:11 reinforces this truth, promising that God will not withhold any good thing from those who live uprightly. In this chapter, I will share keys to unlocking the doors to God's blessings in your life.

Our words are a vital part of this process, as Galatians 6:7 and Jeremiah 1:12 indicate. We must be mindful of our speech, sowing words of blessings and speaking life into our circumstances. Job 22:28 teaches us the power of decreeing things, highlighting the impact of our words on our reality.

However, negative speech can limit what God can do in our lives. Proverbs 18:21 and Ephesians 4:29 caution against corrupt communication, emphasizing the importance of speaking words that edify and minister grace.

To live victoriously, we must cultivate a deep hunger for change and prepare to focus on it. Doing the same thing repeatedly and expecting different results is counterproductive. Numbers 14:28 shows us that God responds to our spoken words, and thus, it's crucial to align our speech with His promises.

In addition to our words, our mindset plays a crucial role. By keeping our thoughts centered on God and meditating on His word, we position ourselves for spiritual success. Hosea 4:6 warns of the dangers of lacking knowledge, emphasizing the importance of immersing ourselves in the Scriptures.

Praying in tongues, as suggested in Romans 8:26-27, is another way to stay attuned to God's presence. This form of prayer allows the Holy Spirit to intercede through us, expressing what we cannot utter ourselves.

Daily elevating Jesus through praise and worship changes our surroundings and rejuvenates our spirit. Even medical professionals have observed the positive impact of worship on patients. Paul and Silas's experience in prison, as recorded in the book of Acts, is a testament to the power of worship in bringing divine intervention.

Proverbs 13:20 reminds us of the importance of wise associations. The company we keep can either enhance or hinder our spiritual growth. It's essential to form relationships that draw us closer to Christ and steer clear of those that pull us away.

Understanding the principle of giving and its rewards is another crucial aspect of living a victorious life. John 3:16, Luke 6:38, and Malachi 3:10-11 highlight the blessings that come with generosity and faithfulness in tithes and offerings. When we give, we align ourselves with God's nature and open ourselves up to His abundant provision.

Understanding the seasons according to God's calendar, as stated in Ecclesiastes 3:1, is vital for timely sowing and reaping. Releasing what we have in faith prompts God to release His blessings upon us.

Living victoriously every day is not just a possibility, it's a promise from God. In this chapter, I aim to inspire you with insights into the profound impact of our words, thoughts, associations, generosity, and the experience of God's favor. These five key areas of spiritual growth, when nurtured, can deepen your relationship with the Lord and lead you towards holistic prosperity.

Mark 10:29-30 and 3 John 1:2 encapsulate God's desire for our prosperity in every aspect of our lives. As you trust and obey Him, you will witness His faithfulness, blessing your life abundantly.

Psalms 84:11 promises that God will not withhold any good thing from those who walk uprightly. In this chapter, I will share keys to unlock the blessings in your life.

Our words have tremendous power, as shown in Galatians 6:7 and Jeremiah 1:12. We can speak life and blessings into our circumstances. Conversely, negative speech can limit what God can do in our lives, as Proverbs 18:21 and Ephesians 4:29 caution us.

The story of the Shunammite woman in 2 Kings 4:8-17 demonstrates the power of hospitality and generosity. Her kindness towards Elisha was rewarded with the miracle of a son, echoing the principle that God honors those who honor Him. Similarly, I've witnessed God's faithfulness in rewarding generosity and hospitality in modern times, as with a couple who, after seventeen years of childlessness, conceived a child following our prayers.

The favor of God can turn ordinary lives into extraordinary testimonies. Esther's story, as narrated in Esther 2:16, is a classic example of how God's favor can elevate someone from obscurity to significance. Remembering Romans 8:31-37, we are assured that with God on our side, we are more than conquerors.

Therefore, I encourage you to expect great things from God. He is capable of doing immeasurably more than we can ask or imagine. My prayer for you is that as you apply these principles in your life, you will thrive physically, financially, emotionally, and spiritually. May you be a vessel of His blessings and a testimony to His immense power and love.

EMBRACING SUPERNATURAL FAVOR

In this dynamic chapter, "The Day of Manifestation: Impartation of Favor," I aim to uplift and empower you to triumphantly pursue your destiny. I will share prophetically about the extraordinary season of favor that is upon the faithful believers today. This favor brings empowerment, greater authority, grace, spiritual blessings, and supernatural provisions for an unprecedented harvest. You'll learn how to delight the Lord and position yourself to receive heavenly anointing, favor, and an overcoming spirit, preparing you to bear abundant fruit.

In the most exciting age for spiritual harvest since Pentecost, we are stepping into a time of divine favor, a season of holy commissioning, empowerment, and an immense outpouring of the Holy Spirit. As foretold, God is showering His chosen saints with blessings, merging the former and latter rains for a bountiful harvest. Those who have walked faithfully but not yet seen their day of increase, favor, and authority will soon step into their destined roles, as exemplified by biblical figures like Jesus and King David.

Luke 2:52 and Luke 1:80 depict the growth of Jesus and John the Baptist in wisdom, stature, and favor. King David's life also illustrates how God's favor can progressively increase, expanding with each stage of faithful, intimate walk with the Lord.

The Holy Spirit imparts that God is crowning His diligent, faithful saints with a crown of favor and authority, bestowing them with greater installments of spiritual blessings. Each faithful step brings a new measure of God's favor, as stated in Hebrews 11:6.

Favor is God's pleasure in His people, leading to spiritual blessings, goodwill, and grace. We are entering a time of increased favor, where God will empower His believers for a significant spiritual harvest. This season is marked by the birthing of ministries and destinies, where God's saints step into the fullness of His grace.

Proverbs 10:22 and 10:4 illustrate that God enriches and favors the diligent. These blessings will manifest as success, authority, and prominence, bringing divine qualifications for extraordinary feats. God is selecting and commissioning His favored ones for greater works, as shown through the example of Esther in Esther 2.

God spoke to me about the "first fruits sons and daughters" who would birth ministries rapidly, a testament to His favor. This season of favor is marked by God granting the desires of those pleasing to Him, as shown in John 15:15 and 15:7. It's a time for preparation and positioning to be pleasing before the King, a time of intimate worship and communion with God.

Aaron's rod, a symbol of authority and favor, blossomed miraculously, indicating God's choice of him as high priest (Psalms 23:4). This season is about God placing the rod of kingship, favor, and authority in the hands of the chosen, resulting in a fruitful and empowered life.

In this season, believers will receive God's commission, backed by heaven, to fulfill their calling fully. The gifts and power manifesting through them will bear witness to God's approval, as Jesus's works bore witness of His divine commission (John 5:19, 30, 36).

This season is about seeing the evidence of God's favor in every aspect of life. The blessings and authority that come with this favor will manifest in significant and impactful ways, leading to the realization of God's promises and an abundant harvest.

My prayer for you is that as you embrace these truths, you will experience the full manifestation of God's favor, bearing witness to His glory through your life and calling.

"The Day of Manifestation: Impartation of Favor," I aim to uplift and empower you to triumphantly pursue your destiny. I will share prophetically about the extraordinary season of favor that is upon the faithful believers today. This favor brings empowerment, greater authority, grace, spiritual blessings, and supernatural provisions for an unprecedented harvest. You'll learn how to delight the Lord and position yourself to receive heavenly anointing, favor, and an overcoming spirit, preparing you to bear abundant fruit.

In the most exciting age for spiritual harvest since Pentecost, we are stepping into a time of divine favor, a season of holy commissioning, empowerment, and an immense outpouring of the Holy Spirit. As foretold, God is showering His chosen saints with blessings, merging the former and latter rains for a bountiful harvest. Those who have walked faithfully but not yet seen their day of increase, favor, and authority will soon step into their destined roles, as exemplified by biblical figures like Jesus and King David.

Luke 2:52 and Luke 1:80 depict the growth of Jesus and John the Baptist in wisdom, stature, and favor. King David's life also illustrates how God's favor can progressively increase, expanding with each stage of faithful, intimate walk with the Lord.

The Holy Spirit imparts that God is crowning His diligent, faithful saints with a crown of favor and authority, bestowing them with greater installments of spiritual blessings. Each faithful step brings a new measure of God's favor, as stated in Hebrews 11:6.

Favor is God's pleasure in His people, leading to spiritual blessings, goodwill, and grace. We are entering a time of increased favor, where God will empower His believers for a significant spiritual harvest. This season is marked by the birthing of ministries and destinies, where God's saints step into the fullness of His grace.

Proverbs 10:22 and 10:4 illustrate that God enriches and favors the diligent. These blessings will manifest as success, authority, and prominence, bringing divine qualifications for extraordinary feats. God is selecting and commissioning His favored ones for greater works, as shown through the example of Esther in Esther 2.

God spoke to me about the "first fruits sons and daughters" who would birth ministries rapidly, a testament to His favor. This season of favor is marked by God granting the desires of those pleasing to Him, as shown in John 15:15 and 15:7. It's a time for preparation and positioning to be pleasing before the King, a time of intimate worship and communion with God.

Aaron's rod, a symbol of authority and favor, blossomed miraculously, indicating God's choice of him as high priest (Psalms 23:4). This season is about God placing the rod of kingship, favor, and authority in the hands of the chosen, resulting in a fruitful and empowered life.

In this season, believers will receive God's commission, backed by heaven, to fulfill their calling fully. The gifts and power manifesting through them will bear witness to God's approval, as Jesus's works bore witness of His divine commission (John 5:19, 30, 36).

This season is about seeing the evidence of God's favor in every aspect of life. The blessings and authority that come with this favor will manifest in significant and impactful ways, leading to the realization of God's promises and an abundant harvest.

My prayer for you is that as you embrace these truths, you will experience the full manifestation of God's favor, bearing witness to His glory through your life and calling.

ACHIEVING FINANCIAL
FREEDOM THROUGH FAITH

In this challenging season, many Christians have found themselves struggling financially. God has placed on my heart a message of hope and empowerment for financial breakthrough. Let's begin with a prayer for liberation from financial bondage and for divine provision.

In the mighty name of Jesus of Nazareth, I stand against all spiritual forces hindering financial prosperity in your life, your family, friends, and church community. I rebuke the influence of false gods, particularly Baal, that mislead and control people's perspectives on wealth. I declare freedom from the spirit of mammon, which fosters unrighteousness, bitterness, and a distorted focus on money.

Matthew 6:24 reminds us that we cannot serve both God and mammon. Our allegiance and trust must be solely in God, our ultimate provider. Philippians 4:19 assures us of God's commitment to meet all our needs according to His glorious riches in

Christ Jesus. Therefore, as Matthew 6:31 advises, we should not be consumed by worries about our material needs.

I break the chains of negative mindsets surrounding money: the fear of not having enough, impulse buying, greed, discontentment, the bondage of debt, and the excessive importance placed on financial wealth. I dispel any spirits of greed, covetousness, and manipulation related to money, as well as the spirit of depression that can emerge from financial worries.

God promises that the wealth of the wicked is stored up for the righteous (Proverbs 13:22). Therefore, I pray for a spirit of faithful stewardship. May we be diligent in sowing seeds, giving offerings, and tithing to our local churches. Lord, transform us into wise managers of money for Your Kingdom's purposes, reminding us that money is a tool to serve us in fulfilling Your will, not for us to serve it.

Lord Jesus, I ask You to ignite our faith in the area of giving. Make us accountable with our finances, opening our ears to Your guidance and our eyes to Your wisdom. Release upon us a spirit of discernment and wisdom where finances are concerned.

In Jesus' Name, Amen.

This prayer encapsulates our desire for financial freedom through faith. It's a reminder that our focus should not be on wealth itself, but on using what God provides for His glory and the advancement of His Kingdom. As we align our financial practices with God's principles, we open the doors to His blessings and provision.

EMBRACING GOD'S DREAMS

After experiencing unfulfilled dreams for years, I discovered the transformative power of dreaming with God. Embracing this concept can revolutionize your life. When we dare to envision things far beyond our capabilities, rooted in God's Word, embodying Christ's heart, and aimed solely at glorifying Him, God enters the scene magnificently. Now, more than ever, as individuals and collectively as the Body of Christ, we need visions that transcend our limitations, visions that demand God's divine intervention. Without a God-inspired vision, souls remain unreached, and destinies unfulfilled.

Salvation is a matter of the heart, and so are visions. They reflect Christ's heart and our faith in Him. As Philippians 2:3-5 instructs, we should adopt the mindset of Christ, looking beyond our interests to the needs of others. Visions are essential for our faith journey, challenging us to adopt Christ's heart for the lost and to believe beyond our human abilities.

God prioritizes the future over the past. He has an ultimate plan that surpasses our understanding, involving the fulfillment of His original intent for creation. When we open ourselves to God-sized dreams, we step into a realm of new possibilities far exceeding our expectations. Trust that when God imparts a vision, He also provides the means to achieve it.

God challenges us: Do we see Him as the supernatural, almighty God, capable of orchestrating extraordinary, incomprehensible acts today, or not? We can no longer shy away from this question – He deserves our answer. He's calling for a faithful, radical remnant, united beyond creed, race, rank, and age, with a shared passion for lost souls and revival. This culture of spiritual awakening is characterized by an understanding of the times and a preparedness to embrace God's ultimate plan.

The urgency for soul-winning has never been more critical. Whether it's an individual, a family, a city, or a nation, we need the visionary insight that Apostle Paul had – to hear the cry of humanity and respond as he did to the Macedonian call. As in Acts 16, this response can lead to earth-shaking revivals, spiritual liberations, and widespread transformations.

My journey with God has been one of deep immersion in His Word and presence, leading to dreams about preaching and bringing healing. Emptied of self, I opened my heart to Christ's purposes, resulting in a burning passion for the lost. God's dreams are invariably grander than ours. My prayer for multitudes led to God revealing even greater plans – a vision for winning a million souls!

Deuteronomy 8:18 reminds us that it is God who empowers us to achieve wealth and fulfill His covenant. Visions are first planted in our hearts, the dwelling place of Christ, where faith and assurance reside. I embraced this vision for a million souls, pushing beyond my mind's limitations, and witnessed its manifestation through God's power.

In the early days of my ministry, I relied solely on the treasure He gave us – the vision. I witnessed God's power in drawing people to us, leading to miraculous healings, salvations, and transformations. These beginnings, though small, were founded on big, Holy Spirit-inspired dreams for God's great exploits.

I urge you not to cease dreaming and to dream boldly. With God, even the impossible becomes possible, advancing His Kingdom. We need vast visions for souls, aligned with Christ's heart. As He showed compassion for the multitudes, so must we.

The importance of time spent with Jesus, in His Word, prayer, and worship, cannot be overstated. In these moments, He prepares our hearts for vision planting. Dreams and visions are the Holy Spirit's love language to us. Immersed in His presence, I felt compelled to take Christ's message to the world.

My prayer is for the cross of Christ to be etched deeply in our hearts, individually and collectively, driving us to reach the lost. As Habakkuk 1:5 declares, God is set to accomplish a work in our days that is beyond belief.

God's vision for Revival Waves of Glory is an unprecedented harvest of souls. I am committed to this vision, believing that our first million souls are just the beginning. Dreaming with God, I trust Him to lead us according to His will. Our heart for the harvest aligns with His Word and advances His Kingdom.

My dream is to ignite evangelistic zeal in God's people, to bring Christ's Gospel and the Holy Spirit's power into every corner of society. Jesus empowered His disciples for this work, and He empowers us too. This power extends to all whom God calls.

I eagerly anticipate tomorrow because of the promise of God's power and presence in our mission. Great exploits await us – whether in stadiums, pulpits, our backyards, or online. The fields are ripe for harvest, and with God's provision, our biggest dreams can become

We are currently experiencing a season of remarkable acceleration, and I am profoundly grateful for your prayers, support, and partnership. This phase resonates deeply with the spirit of

Matthew 10:7-8, where Jesus instructs, "As you go, preach, saying, 'The kingdom of heaven is at hand. Heal the sick, cleanse the lepers, raise the dead, cast out devils: freely you have received, freely give.'"

These words encapsulate our mission and drive. As we journey forward, our focus is steadfast on proclaiming the imminent presence of God's kingdom. This message is not just in word, but also in action – healing the sick, bringing restoration and life, and liberating those bound by oppression. The essence of our ministry is rooted in the principle of giving freely, echoing the generosity we have received from the Lord.

Our commitment is to advance with this message, propelled by the swift winds of God's Spirit. This acceleration is not just a matter of pace but of depth and impact. As we navigate this dynamic season, we recognize the increased need for divine guidance, wisdom, and strength. Therefore, your continual support through prayer is invaluable. It fortifies us, enabling us to move in alignment with God's will and purpose.

Furthermore, your partnership in this journey is more than mere assistance; it is a shared venture in the kingdom's work. As we collectively heed the call to bring healing, restoration, and the message of the Gospel, we are fulfilling the great commission entrusted to us by Jesus Christ.

This season of acceleration calls for a deeper reliance on the Holy Spirit and a greater commitment to the mission. Let us remain steadfast, embracing this divine momentum, and together, we will witness the unfolding of God's kingdom on earth as it is in heaven. Your role in this endeavor is deeply appreciated, and together, we shall see the manifestation of God's power and glory in unprecedented ways.

EMBRACING DIVINE ALLIANCES FOR GOD'S PURPOSE

The formation of alliances, under God's guidance, is a strategic element in fulfilling His purpose. Emphasized in Psalms 133:1-3, the psalmist David celebrates the beauty and benefits of brethren dwelling together in unity. It's compared to precious anointing oil, symbolizing blessing and consecration, and it's this spirit of unity that the enemy tirelessly attempts to disrupt.

In these challenging times, our survival and growth are anchored in our willingness to form God-centered alliances. These alliances, rooted in trust and mutual support, become indispensable in ministries and communities thriving in faith.

An alliance, in its essence, is a commitment to a mutual goal, underpinned by shared values and visions. It's an agreement to advance a common cause, which, for us as Christians of the 21st century, is the advancement of God's Kingdom and the spreading of the Gospel of Jesus Christ.

Our world, now more than ever, is searching for answers amidst chaos. As the Church, it's our responsibility to lead by example, showcasing unity and cooperation. The emerging era calls for divine alliances that transcend personal ambitions, aligning with a higher calling that unites believers in a singular, God-driven mission.

In the Bible, we see instances of successful divine alliances as well as cautionary tales of unholy alliances that displeased God. The key differentiator is the foundation of these alliances – whether they are built on godly principles or on compromise and idolatry.

A prime biblical example of a godly alliance is the bond between David and Jonathan, as seen in 1 Samuel 20:42. Their alliance was grounded in mutual respect, trust, and a shared vision for Israel's future. It exemplifies how divine alliances can lead to personal survival and national welfare.

The New Testament also showcases alliances, like that of Paul and Barnabas, which were pivotal in the spread of the Gospel post-Pentecost. These partnerships were not forced but naturally formed under divine guidance, highlighting the importance of being equally yoked in vision and spirit.

In 2 Peter 1:5-8, we're reminded of the importance of fraternal affection and brotherly love as cornerstones in our journey to become one with the Lord. These virtues are vital in forging alliances that are not just effective but also reflective of Christ's love and compassion.

As we look to form alliances in ministry and life, we must seek God's guidance to connect with those who align with His purpose for us. These partnerships, when formed under His blessing, can lead to unprecedented growth, safety, and impact.

In conclusion, divine alliances are not just strategic partnerships but spiritual connections that resonate with God's heart. As we commit to these relationships, we unlock blessings and opportunities, advancing the Kingdom of God with unity and purpose.

EMBRACING THE CHANGING SEASONS OF FAITH

Every Christian journey is marked by seasons of change, guided by the Holy Spirit's anointing. The sons of Issachar, as mentioned in 1 Chronicles 12:32, were known for their deep understanding of times and seasons, and their ability to discern what Israel ought to do. Emulating this wisdom in discerning God's voice and aligning our actions with His guidance can bring transformative change in our lives.

We often sense God's voice, but understanding and acting upon His directions is a different challenge. When we align with God's word, we see the natural world responding to His divine command.

The present time, as I perceive, is not about warfare but about victories and advancements. It's a season of greater glory, emerging from times of corporate and individual shaking. While some might still be in the throes of struggle, I declare a season of blessings, breakthroughs, and favor, with a call to build and progress.

However, there are times of preparation, signified by red lights from the Spirit, when we are not called to expand but to re-structure and maintain. I've experienced such seasons myself, times of financial restraint and personal pruning, which, though challenging, were necessary for spiritual growth.

Yet, now, a wind of change is blowing. It's a time for greater blessings and divine advancements. This is the time to build, echoing the Lord's directive. But remember, the green light from God doesn't always signal a call to action. Apostle Paul experienced such divine redirections, as seen in Acts 16:6, where he was stopped from preaching in Asia but later received a vision to minister in Macedonia.

Discerning the right season is crucial. When God signals a green light, it's a call to be fruitful and multiply, to actualize the dreams He plants in our hearts. Our obedience and action in these times honor God, showcasing our faith in His providence and power.

Understanding the right timing is key. With the current call to build, there's a sense of urgency, a quickening by the Holy Spirit to act swiftly, aware that future seasons may bring different directives.

In this season of building, stay focused and avoid distractions. The enemy's tool of distraction can derail us from God's path. As stated in John 9:4, we must work while it is day, for night comes when no work can be done. Declare this season as one of open heavens, greater glory, and advancement. Embrace the call to build and move forward with determination.

When the green light shines, ask God about the timing. Respond promptly and with conviction, as guided by the Holy Spirit. Be prepared for change, as nothing remains constant. Expand your vision, trust in God's provision, and be ready for transformation.

In practical terms, building a vision requires structure and resources. It's essential to take the first steps in faith, trusting

God to guide and provide. The Bible is rich with examples of how God cast His vision through saints like Abraham, Zechariah, and Nehemiah. Their stories offer keys to starting and advancing God's vision.

Abraham's story, in particular, illustrates the power of faith in action. Despite uncertainties, he obeyed God's call (Genesis 15:1-4), setting an example for us to follow. As you embark on your spiritual journey, remember Abraham's faith and trust in God's promise.

Embrace the changing seasons of your faith journey. Whether in times of preparation or action, seek God's guidance and align your steps with His will. Build, expand, and move forward in faith, for with God, all things are possible.

God often calls us to envision His grand designs, as He did with Abram. In Genesis 15:5, He invited Abram to gaze upon the stars and imagine his descendants as numerous as them. This moment wasn't just about counting stars; it was about embracing a vision so vast that it surpassed human comprehension. Here, Abram took the crucial first step: he believed in God's vision.

When God unfolds a vision before us, it's an invitation to dream and to trust. It's about meditating on His promises and allowing ourselves to have "Holy Ghost-sanctified fantasies" about what He is speaking into our lives. The key is to believe in the vision God imparts to our hearts.

Let's explore how God moved Zerubbabel from step one, believing, to step two, acting. In Zechariah Chapters 1-3, God used the prophet Zechariah to provide guidance, encouragement, and confirmation to Zerubbabel during the reconstruction of the Second Temple. Despite the hindrances that stalled the construction (Ezra Chapter Four), Zerubbabel was reinvigorated through prophetic words, igniting a divine fear and a collective spirit to resume work.

The prophets Haggai and Zechariah played a crucial role in this process. They provided not only encouragement but also divine insight that was essential for the project's success. Ezra 6:14 highlights how the elders of the Jews prospered through their prophesying. This underscores an important principle in spiritual endeavors: the necessity of prophetic guidance. Without it, ministries can become stagnant, lacking the dynamic direction that prophecy brings.

An apostolic and prophetic culture is vital for successful spiritual enterprises. Ephesians 2:20 emphasizes that the church is built on the foundation of apostles and prophets, with Jesus Christ Himself as the cornerstone. These roles are designed to complement each other, fostering a dynamic and forward-moving body of Christ.

Nehemiah's story exemplifies the qualities of a true apostolic leader. His reaction to the news of Jerusalem's walls being in ruins (Nehemiah 1:1-4) was not just grief but a call to action. He recognized the need for divine favor and embarked on a journey of fasting, prayer, and strategic planning. His request to the king to rebuild Jerusalem wasn't just a plea; it was a well-thought-out plan fueled by divine inspiration and personal commitment.

Fasting and praying are crucial for victory in spiritual battles. They align our hearts with God's and equip us for the challenges ahead. Nehemiah's approach, combining prayer with practical action, is a model for us today. He wasn't deterred by his position as a cupbearer; instead, he saw an opportunity to make a difference. His readiness to act, bolstered by the king's favor, highlights the importance of divine backing in our endeavors.

In Nehemiah 2:4-5, we see how Nehemiah seized the moment to present his vision to the king. His story teaches us that no matter our background or current position, we can be instrumental in God's plans when we align our desires with His will and act upon them.

God's visions for us are meant to be believed and acted upon. They often start as divine inspirations that challenge our conventional thinking and push us to dream beyond our limitations. Whether it's Abram counting the stars or Nehemiah envisioning the reconstruction of Jerusalem's walls, the common thread is a deep trust in God's promises and the courage to act on them. Let us embrace our divine visions with faith and action, trusting that God will guide and provide every step of the way.

Nehemiah's story is a compelling example of embracing a divine call. He requested letters from the king to ensure safe passage to Judah for a monumental task – rebuilding Jerusalem's walls.

Nehemiah 2:7-9 depicts his strategic approach, securing not just the king's written endorsement but also military support. This narrative underscores a vital aspect of apostolic calling: it's not about your current role or status. Whether you're a cupbearer like Nehemiah or in any other profession, if you are called by God, you are equipped for the task. An apostolic individual is driven by a vision to restore and rejuvenate what has been broken.

Nehemiah's journey to Jerusalem was not just physical but also a journey of faith and vision. Upon arrival, he quietly assessed the situation (Nehemiah 2:12) and then shared his vision with the people, igniting a collective determination to rebuild (Nehemiah 2:18).

However, undertaking God's work often invites opposition. Nehemiah 4:1-12 illustrates this, as enemies mocked and plotted against the rebuilding efforts. Yet, Nehemiah's divine strategy, including setting armed workers and alert systems, thwarted these attempts. His response to distractions and threats, as seen in Nehemiah 6:2-4, highlights a crucial lesson: stay focused on your God-given task. Distractions, whether negative or seemingly positive, must not deter you from your divine assignment.

This story is not just about rebuilding walls; it's about the unwavering commitment to a God-given vision, regardless of external challenges. It teaches us to be steadfast in our purpose, resilient in the face of opposition, and focused on our divine calling.

As we reflect on Nehemiah's story, let's remember that the call to rebuild can manifest in various forms in our lives. It could be a call to restore relationships, rebuild communities, or even to revive our spiritual fervor. The key is to respond with faith, strategic planning, and an unyielding focus on the task at hand.

So, let us take inspiration from Nehemiah's journey. Let's be open to God's call, ready to rise to challenges, and prepared to stay the course until the work is complete. Remember, when God calls you to a task, He equips you with everything you need to accomplish it. Your role is to stay committed, focused, and faithful to that calling.

UNLEASHING BREAKTHROUGH REVIVAL

The term 'revival' has often been diluted in its usage, but its true essence is about to be powerfully reinstated. Prophetic insights have revealed the presence of an angel named "Breakthrough," specifically assigned to usher in a wave of revival across the United States. This angel, known for his role in historic revivals, is set to catalyze a spiritual awakening, clearing obstacles to God's plan and aiding in the gathering of souls.

God has disclosed that groundwork for this upcoming revival has been underway for two years. This revival, it seems, will be so immense that current stadiums will struggle to accommodate the multitudes it attracts.

The misconception that God only speaks during extended periods of prayer and fasting is being challenged. The Lord is known to communicate even amidst turmoil, exhaustion, or trials. The nature of angelic messengers varies; while some may appear formidable, others exude gentleness and compassion. These end-time provision angels congregate where God is actively moving.

Jesus' explanation in Matthew 13:37-43 about the end times is crucial to understanding the spiritual dynamics at play. The field (the world) where both good and bad seeds (the children of the kingdom and the wicked one, respectively) have been sown is approaching harvest time, with angels playing a pivotal role in separating the wheat from the chaff.

The coming revival will not be defined by human wisdom or might but through an intimate understanding of God, as emphasized in Jeremiah 9:23-24. This period is about mobilizing the Body of Christ to act as intermediaries on Earth, as outlined in Zechariah 12:8, which promises that even the weakest believer will exhibit the strength and victory akin to King David.

The strategy for this end-time revival involves a fusion of heavenly and earthly efforts. This approach mirrors King David's experience with the Philistines in 2 Samuel 5. David awaited a sign – the sound of wind in the balsam trees – to initiate his victorious attack. Similarly, believers must learn to discern and act upon these divine timings and strategies.

Hebrews 1:7 highlights the role of angels as both spiritual beings and ministers of fire, indicating a cooperative relationship between the heavenly host and the church. Understanding and acting upon spiritual insights are key to activating the resources and strategies allocated to us.

The birthing of Judah's twins, described in Genesis 38:27-30, serves as a metaphor for the church's role in this revival. We are called to be bold and resolute, not shrinking back in fear or opposition but pressing forward to witness the fulfillment of God's promises (Hebrews 10:37-39).

In conclusion, we stand at a critical juncture in church history, a 'fullness of time' moment where God's end-time plan is unfolding. Our response should be a renewed devotion to Christ and a commitment to prayer, empowering the spiritual host to battle for us. Despite the evident troubles in our world, God's grace abounds even more. We are called to seize this divine opportunity, utilizing the remarkable gifts and resources provided at this pivotal time.

BIRTHING CHAMPIONS
FOR GOD

In this pivotal hour, a new breed of dedicated saints is emerging, ready to become champions for God. This season is characterized by a profound spiritual awakening, as prophesied in Micah 4:9-10. Here, the labor pains and the process of birth symbolize the emergence of spiritual champions, called to express the heart and power of the Great Champion of Heaven through their lives.

Moses, for instance, abandoned Egypt's opulence to embrace the identity and struggles of God's people, setting a spiritual precedent. True spiritual victory comes from completely yielding to Jesus and representing Heaven on Earth. Just as God chose Israel and within Israel, the tribe of Levi, and further within Levi, the descendants of Zadok, there's a pattern of a remnant within a remnant. This faithful core, devoted even in times of spiritual decline, receives God's grace and favor, empowering them to become Heaven's representatives on Earth.

In these times of confusion, akin to Babylon, a victorious body of believers, embodying the traits of "overcomers," will emerge.

The Bible speaks of God's zealous desire for the anointing He places within us (James 4:5). His Spirit delves into the depths of His heart, unveiling the secrets of His plans and purposes for this generation.

God has measured a specific period to execute His redemption plan, foreseeing the end from the beginning. He foresaw not only the ancient patriarchs but also the end-time leaders, imbuing a chosen generation with a destiny seed. This generation is destined to emerge at the end of time to become Heaven's champions. Before shaping the Earth, He envisioned an "overcoming" generation, embodying His nature and power, and set forth a victory plan we are now beginning to experience.

The encounter of Jesus with the Samaritan woman at the well, as narrated in John 4, is a profound spiritual reality with direct relevance today. This woman, unknown by name, had a life-changing, face-to-face encounter with the King of Glory. This pivotal day marked a transformation not just for her but also for her entire city. Each day of Jesus' earthly life was divinely orchestrated by the Holy Spirit, making this encounter a deliberate strategy to awaken the destiny within this woman.

Before the world's foundation, a destiny seed was planted in her, which Jesus awakened through His revelatory knowledge. This encounter is a prophetic model for the Western Church's awakening in this era. The Western Church, like the Samaritan woman, has been entangled in various allegiances, neglecting her true purpose. Now, the time has come for the seeds of destiny to be ignited, following the pattern set in John Chapter 4.

Jesus' use of revelatory knowledge to reveal the woman's heart is the key to awakening the Western Church to its destiny. Our transformation into spiritual champions depends on an impartation from Heaven, allowing the Lord to manifest His virtues and character through us. The woman's transformation into an evangelist, sparked by supernatural faith, is a model for the church's awakening to win our nation.

Like the Samaritan woman, the hidden seeds of destiny in today's generation will be ignited by the Living Word. The revelatory realm of Heaven, discerning the thoughts and intents of the heart, will awaken these seeds, leading to a harvest of spiritual champions.

This woman's encounter with Jesus at the well transformed her into a powerful evangelist, her testimony awakening her entire city. Our mission is to identify and nurture the hidden seeds of destiny in today's champions. They may not currently appear as champions, but like the Samaritan woman, they carry a destiny that will be stirred to spiritual greatness. It is through the Living Word, revealing and discerning the heart's thoughts and intentions, that this revelatory realm of Heaven will come to fruition.

As the Lord's light strikes the seeds of destiny in people, it will awaken them to a victorious life, and an army of champions will emerge. The revelatory light of His end-time plan is now igniting souls, transforming them into the champions they were ordained to be.

APOSTOLIC REVOLUTION

In this transformative era, God is orchestrating an apostolic revolution within the Body of Christ, heralding a new era of Church governance. Across America, God is fostering the rise of apostolic centers, far beyond traditional church planting. Revival Waves of Glory is at the forefront of this movement, pioneering what I believe will be the first of many such centers nationwide.

These apostolic centers represent a profound shift in spiritual dynamics. As I've traveled, the Holy Spirit has impressed upon me the importance of prophesying about these centers and envisioning their impact. Many believers are being called to engage in this monumental shift, to be part of something far greater than what we've known. This could mean the emergence of a center in your locality, inviting you to play a pivotal role.

Despite being amidst God's move, many believers are yet to recognize its onset. Acknowledging and understanding this movement is critical for us to assume greater responsibility within it. My aim is to outline a prophetic framework to help us grasp and contribute effectively to this divine wave, which encompasses healing, prayer movements, and evangelism. This synthesis signifies a greater global move, likely under the apostolic banner, which transcends conventional boundaries and definitions.

The term 'apostolic' is frequently bandied about in church circles, often without a clear understanding of its implications for church structure and function. It's about more than just terminology; it signifies a fundamental transformation in how we 'do' church. As this new model takes shape, it will bring specific anointings necessary for its fruition.

To genuinely embrace the apostolic call, one must understand what it embodies. An apostle, essentially a Christian faith missionary or a proponent of significant moral reform, must be divinely appointed. This distinction between God-made and man-made apostles is crucial. True apostles are prepared, anointed, and sent by God, not self-appointed or designated by human institutions. While God restores apostolic figures in the church, caution is advised against self-proclaimed apostles. Often, the genuine ones are recognized by their anointing rather than their claims.

In the context of prophetic reception (Matthew 10:41), it's important to recognize that not all prophets are universally accepted, as their ministry may be specific to certain groups. Similarly, apostles and evangelists have their distinct spheres of influence. To wield the title 'apostle', one should ideally demonstrate miraculous signs and wonders.

Let's explore nine key characteristics of genuine apostolic anointing and authority:

1. **Separation:** Apostles lead lives of consecration and are wholly dedicated to God's purposes (Romans 1:1).
2. **Fathering:** They possess a nurturing spirit, fostering spiritual maturity in others (1 Corinthians 4:15).
3. **Team Counsel:** Apostles embrace collaborative efforts and value wisdom from various sources (Acts 15:6).

4. **Signs, Wonders, and Perseverance:** Their ministry is marked by enduring faith and miraculous deeds (2 Corinthians 12:12).
5. **Humility:** True apostles exhibit humility, following Paul's example (Philippians 2:3; 1 Corinthians 15:9).
6. **Servanthood:** They prioritize service to Christ and others, as Paul did (1 Corinthians 11:1).
7. **Revelatory Gifting:** Apostles receive and preach the gospel through divine revelation (Galatians 1:11-12).
8. **Building Networks:** They focus on establishing a network of churches and ministries, fostering unity and collaborative growth.
9. **Global Influence:** Apostles have a vision that extends beyond local boundaries, influencing the global church and its mission.

In summary, the apostolic revolution is not just about new structures or systems; it's a radical reformation of how we perceive and operate within the Body of Christ. It's about embracing a new wave of God's movement, characterized by divine anointing, supernatural works, and a global vision. As we step into this new era, let us align ourselves with God's vision and become active participants in this transformative apostolic revolution.

God is calling for apostles of unimpeachable character, trustworthy bearers of life-altering missions affecting multitudes. His strategy involves an intense character-building process, marked by trials and tribulations, to sculpt apostles who truly reflect His heart. These ordeals, though challenging, foster perseverance, character, and hope, aligning with Paul's teachings in Romans 5:3-5. Apostles enduring this process emerge equipped with a message of hope and salvation, their refined character earning them God's favor and a good name, as prized as great riches (Proverbs 22:1).

Apostolic Breakthrough

Modern apostles mirror Paul's pioneering spirit, venturing into unexplored territories to spread the gospel (Romans 15:20-21). They thrive on the adventure of new frontiers, driven by a kingly authority to expand God's kingdom powerfully.

Intercession and Evangelism: The Apostolic Movement

Jesus revealed to me a crucial insight: the interlocking nature of the prayer and evangelism movements is essential for unleashing the great harvest. These movements, part of the overarching apostolic movement, culminate in revival. The restoration of the Tabernacle of David, symbolizing perpetual worship and intercession, is pivotal to this process. This understanding aligns with James' interpretation in Acts 15:16 of the burgeoning harvest.

The revival and harvest are inherently connected to the restoration of continuous prayer, as prophesied in Amos 9:11-13. This burgeoning prayer movement, mirroring the early church's devotion to prayer (Acts 2:47), is the precursor to an unprecedented healing revival and a global harvest of souls.

Healing Revival

The forthcoming healing revival, foretold in Malachi 4:1-2, will manifest through God's power. Just as Peter's shadow brought healing in Acts 5:15-16, modern apostles will carry a presence so potent that healing occurs in their very vicinity.

This revival, marked by repentance and restoration, will reinvigorate the church with evangelistic fervor and miraculous signs (2 Chronicles 7:14-15). It signals a time of accelerated spiritual growth and harvest, as described in Amos 6:4.

Forerunners of Revival

God's strategy includes sending apostles and prophets as forerunners, echoing John the Baptist and Elijah's roles. These modern-day forerunners, endowed with the Elijah anointing, are already at work, preparing the ground for a mighty move of God. This anointing, linked with healing and revival, was misunderstood in Jesus' time (Matthew 17:10) but is now manifesting powerfully in today's church.

The Elijah anointing will empower end-time believers to perform miraculous works, shaking cities and nations, as prophesied in Malachi 4:5. This chapter aims to provide a clear vision of the impending healing revival and the pivotal role of apostolic leadership in ushering in this transformative era.

We are witnessing a pivotal era, echoing the days of Acts and Amos, where a great harvest looms on the horizon. This chapter explores the dynamic shift in apostolic authority and identity that God is orchestrating in His Church.

A striking biblical example of this transformation is found in the relationship between Barnabas and Saul. Initially, it was always "Barnabas and Saul" (Acts 11:30, 12:25, 13:1-2). However, a significant change occurred during a service when the Holy Spirit instructed their separation for His work (Acts 13:2). This divinely ordained moment led to a renaming: Saul became Paul, and henceforth, it was "Paul and Barnabas" (Acts 13:13). This shift exemplifies the kind of apostolic reordering God intends for today.

The apostle's role, as a "sent one" and messenger, emerges not from human will but divine ordination. Today, many claim apostolic titles without exhibiting the true signs of apostolic anointing. Authentic apostles, often reluctant to bear the title, demonstrate their calling through tangible fruit and impact, not just words. They embody humility, seeking recognition not in titles but in the anointing and fruit of their ministry.

God is heralding a new governance in the Church, moving away from traditional structures dominated by boards or pastoral hierarchies. This emerging apostolic framework involves a collaborative team ministry, integrating apostles, prophets, pastors, teachers, evangelists, and other ministry gifts in a spirit of unity and mutual respect.

In this new model, competition gives way to camaraderie, and the Church's leadership is marked by relational integrity and spiritual discernment. Senior pastors will collaborate with their prophetic, teaching, and apostolic counterparts, fostering a diverse yet harmonious leadership. Local churches will continue, but their governance will evolve, aligning more closely with apostolic centers that embody this new model.

Although this transition presents challenges due to its novelty and lack of established language, there is a palpable readiness among believers to embrace God's unfolding plan. This willingness to engage with the unknown, to say "Yes!" to God's movements, reflects a deep hunger for spiritual gifts, mantles, anointing, and divine commissioning.

We stand on the brink of a significant shift, akin to the transition from "Barnabas and Saul" to "Paul and Barnabas." It signifies a change in identity, position, influence, and divine promotion. God is preparing His Church for a new level of apostolic authority and impact, rewarding those who earnestly seek Him.

As we navigate these transformative times, let us wholeheartedly commit to this apostolic movement. Let us echo the sentiment, "Here I am, Lord, send me." Our readiness to embrace this change, to don new spiritual garments, signifies our participation in an extraordinary move of God, marked by a profound redefinition of apostolic identity and authority.

APOSTOLIC BREAKTHROUGH AND THE POWER OF DECREES

In this season, a higher realm of authority is emerging through apostolic breakthroughs. Apostolic declarations, commissioned in heaven and ordained by God, carry immense power to enact His justice and dismantle the enemy's plans. These declarations, when spoken with divine anointing, unleash a pre-emptive strike against destructive forces.

The Lord is highlighting the significance of apostolic declarations, drawing attention to key scriptures like Isaiah 61:2, which mandates us to proclaim the acceptable year of the LORD and the day of God's vengeance. This anointing empowers us to declare freedom, bringing everything into divine order, like the laws of gravity, setting into motion a force that aligns our lives with God's will.

When we declare under the anointing, it's as if we are echoing Moses and Isaiah, commanding the heavens and earth to witness the power of God's word (Deuteronomy 32:1, Isaiah 1:2).

This declaration of "Jubilee" brings about total deliverance, debt cancellation, and liberation from all forms of bondage.

Furthermore, the declaration of God's favor transforms our surroundings. A moment without this power is followed by a sudden endowment of divine favor, akin to a tangible coat descending from heaven. This favor, synonymous with grace, can significantly change our circumstances.

The release of favor is tied to our pursuit of God. The more passionately we seek Him, the greater the favor we attract. This principle is evident in the lives of biblical figures like Jesus and King David, who grew in favor with both God and man through their devotion and obedience.

A crucial aspect of apostolic declarations is the proclamation of God's vindication in the face of injustice. We are called to declare God's judgment against the forces that oppose His will. This involves accessing the heavenly court system, where the Holy Spirit advocates on our behalf.

Understanding the divine council and counsel is key to grasping how our decrees impact the heavenly realm. The divine council consists of God, angelic hosts, the cloud of witnesses, living prophets, the twelve disciples, the 24 elders, and even demonic forces. In sessions of divine counsel, wisdom and strategies are exchanged.

In the New Testament, the apostle John provides a vivid depiction of the throne room in heaven, revealing the presence of the Trinity and the twenty-four elders. This throne room serves both as a place of worship and a courtroom for judgment.

Daniel's vision complements John's revelation by presenting a detailed image of the throne room, showcasing the Ancient of Days and the Son of Man in their governmental authority.

The power of apostolic declarations is a key element in God's plan for this era. These decrees, when made in alignment with God's will and anointing, have the power to enact significant changes in the spiritual and natural realms. As bearers of this apostolic mantle, we are entrusted with the responsibility to declare God's will boldly, ushering in breakthroughs and divine order in our lives and the world around us.

Daniel's vision in Daniel 7:9-10 reveals a majestic scene of divine judgment presided over by the Ancient of Days, with thousands ministering and multitudes standing before Him as the books of judgment are opened. This scene is complemented by John's and Ezekiel's depictions of the throne of God, each presenting unique perspectives. John describes a throne set upon a sea of glass, while Ezekiel envisions a moving throne on wheels, surrounded by living creatures. These visions symbolize the dynamic presence of God, reminiscent of the Ark of the Covenant carried by Levites, signifying God's moving presence (1 Chronicles 15:2).

The divine council room or heavenly court, situated in the Throne Room, serves as the locus for divine judgments and as a space for worship. This court is not just limited to holy beings; it can also include demonic entities, as illustrated in 1 Kings 22:19-23, where a deceiving spirit participates in the divine council to fulfill God's will.

This understanding of the divine council underscores our role in partnering with God's judicial system. Believers like Joshua and Jeremiah, have historically accessed this realm, standing in God's council to declare His judgments (Zechariah 3:7, Jeremiah 23:18-20). As ambassadors of Christ, we too are called to make heavenly decrees, aligning our proclamations with God's will to release breakthroughs and divine justice.

Apostolic declarations carry the weight of divine authority. When we decree as instructed by God, we align with His justice, setting in motion His plans on earth. The concept of Jubilee, as anointed by God, can be invoked to declare deliverance, debt cancellation, and freedom from bondage. Similarly, declarations of favor can bring about transformations in circumstances, attracting divine grace and favor.

However, these declarations are not just about pronouncing blessings; they also involve engaging in spiritual warfare and seeking justice against the adversary. By standing in the counsel of the Lord, we can make righteous judgments against the forces of darkness, defending the oppressed and needy, as exhorted in Psalms 82:1-8.

The heavenly court system, as seen in the visions of Daniel, John, and Ezekiel, is both a place of divine strategy and a courtroom where judgments are made. Our participation in this system, through prophetic decrees, activates the angelic host to execute God's will on earth. Failure to do so hinders divine intervention in our lives and the lives of others.

As members of God's divine council, we are empowered to decree His will on earth. This responsibility involves not only declaring blessings but also making kingly judgments against injustice and the enemy's plans. As we faithfully execute this role, we partner with the heavenly host to bring about God's kingdom on earth, echoing the prophetic declarations of Job, David, and other biblical figures who understood the power of the spoken word in aligning with God's divine plan.

In our journey of faith, we often encounter moments of challenge and adversity. These moments call for a deeper understanding of the power vested in our words, especially when speaking life, healing, and freedom into situations of despair and captivity. The struggle lies not in the words we utter, but in the belief that underpins them. Our faith in the divine authority of our declarations is pivotal.

The Scriptures remind us that our utterances, when aligned with God's will, hold immense power. Job 22:28 emphasizes this: "Thou shalt also decree a thing, and it shall be established unto thee." Yet, there's a critical need for a deeper comprehension of how to effectively wield this power. Our declarations must be more than words; they need to be faith-filled proclamations that release God's healing and liberating power.

Daniel 7:21-22 gives us insight into the spiritual warfare we face, showing us that the battle is not only in the physical realm but also in the spiritual. The Ancient of Days, representing divine justice and authority, is the one who ultimately grants victory to the saints. This passage encourages us to confidently approach God's throne, knowing that He is just and will act on behalf of His people.

In this battle for justice and freedom, our role is not passive. Psalms 82 challenges us to rise to the occasion, to be the voice for the oppressed, the poor, and the needy. Our decrees should echo God's heart for justice and mercy.

Understanding the power of apostolic declarations, we are called to proclaim God's favor and justice. Isaiah 61:2 embodies this mandate, empowering us to declare the year of the Lord's favor and the day of His vengeance. When we speak with the authority given to us, we enable the angelic realm to act on these declarations, bringing about change in the natural realm.

Our struggle often stems from a lack of belief in the authority we have been given. The challenge is to rise above the physical circumstances and see through the lens of faith. When we proclaim God's truth over situations of injustice, we invite His intervention.

Approaching the heavenly court, we bring before God our cases, trusting in His righteousness and justice. As we present our petitions, we activate the angelic hosts to carry out the decrees we make in alignment with God's will.

This understanding requires a shift in our perspective. Instead of seeing ourselves as victims of circumstances, we must recognize our role as active participants in God's kingdom work. Our declarations of "Restore!" and "Exaltation will come!" are not mere words but powerful tools in the spiritual realm, capable of bringing about divine restoration and breakthrough.

In conclusion, as believers, we are empowered to speak life and freedom into situations of bondage and despair. Our declarations, rooted in faith and aligned with God's will, can shift atmospheres and bring about divine justice and restoration. As we stand firm in our God-given authority, we will see breakthroughs and victories manifest in our lives and the lives of those around us.

SEASON OF GREAT GRACE

We are entering a remarkable period, a season of Great Grace, where God is bestowing upon His people a supernatural level of grace. This Great Grace is a divine empowerment, enabling believers to live victoriously and engage more profoundly in their Christian journey. It's a special anointing from the Holy Spirit, providing believers with the capacity to achieve feats that seem humanly impossible.

Acts 4:33 speaks of this grace vividly: "And with great power gave the apostles witness of the resurrection of the Lord Jesus: and great grace was upon them all." This Great Grace, as described in the Scriptures, serves as a transformative force, bringing grace, favor, and a heightened level of divine assistance, referred to as "great grace" or "grace, grace."

This supernatural grace isn't merely an abstract concept; it's tangible and transferable. It's the divine favor of God, given irrespective of our merits or worth, solely based on His love and kindness. This grace propels us into a realm of divine favor, opening doors and creating opportunities that we may not have earned through our efforts.

The coming season is being proclaimed as "the year of the Lord's favor" (Isaiah 61:2), a time reminiscent of the Jubilee in Scripture. Jubilee symbolizes complete liberation – the cancellation of debts, the release from bondage, and the restoration of properties and relationships. It's a time of divine resetting, where God's grace orchestrates a complete turnaround in our circumstances.

This powerful grace enables us to speak forth prophetic declarations, leading to instantaneous transformations. We can, under God's anointing, proclaim liberty, favor, and Jubilee, setting in motion divine order and blessing.

The Scripture also highlights the life of Samuel, who grew in favor both with the Lord and with men (1 Samuel 2:26). This growth in divine favor is essential and precedes favor with man. The more we align ourselves with God, the more we experience His favor in our lives.

One key to accessing God's favor is through the anointing. Jesus, anointed by God, exemplifies this (Acts 10:38). This anointing, like a spiritual massage, permeates our being, bringing vision, strength, and purpose. It lifts us up, giving us the resilience of a palm tree and the strength of a cedar, enabling us to thrive even in challenging environments.

The anointing also brings about fruitfulness and freshness in our walk with God. We're called to abide in Him, to remain in His presence, which is key to tapping into this anointing. It is in this place of intimate communion with God that we find the strength and favor to fulfill our divine destiny.

In the biblical narrative, David's life is an excellent example of how the anointing can attract divine favor despite challenging circumstances (1 Samuel 22:1-2). David, anointed to be king, had to endure periods of hardship. However, those who recognized the anointing on his life rallied around him, contributing to his eventual rise to kingship.

This story is a powerful reminder that the anointing attracts support, resources, and people. It brings about recognition and partnership, even when outward circumstances may not reflect our calling or potential.

This season of Great Grace is a time of divine empowerment and favor. It's a period where God's supernatural grace will enable us to overcome obstacles, achieve our divine purpose, and experience a significant transformation in our lives. As we step into this season, let us do so with expectancy, ready to receive and walk in the fullness of the great grace that God is pouring out.

The story of Queen Esther is a profound illustration of divine favor. Taken from the safety of her uncle's home, Esther found herself in the royal palace, vying to be the new queen. Her journey began with favor from the palace official, followed by a period of preparation that included six months with oil, symbolizing death, suffering, and sacrifice, and another six months with perfumes, representing the fragrance of Jesus and the presence of God.

Esther's preparation was vital. It was her dedication to purity, her separation for a special purpose, that positioned her for favor with the king. When she eventually stood before him, clad in royal apparel, she found favor in his eyes (Esther 5:1-3). This favor wasn't arbitrary; it was the fruit of her deliberate preparation and her heart's posture towards God.

Esther's story teaches us a crucial lesson about favor and preparation. Like her, we too must prepare ourselves, seeking God with a hunger and desperation. Esther called for a fast, setting herself apart (Esther 4:16). This act of dedication is what we need to embrace if we are to find favor in our own spheres of influence.

Her journey to becoming queen was marked by a divine favor that set her apart from all other women. Yet, it's essential to recognize that God's favor can vary among individuals. Scripture shows us examples of this favoritism: Joseph was favored above his brothers (Genesis 37), and Jacob was favored over Esau (Genesis 27). The key to this favor lies in our relationship with God. A heart passionately seeking Him, like David's, attracts God's favor despite our imperfections and shortcomings.

Now, we are stepping into a season of Great Grace. This is not just ordinary grace but a supernatural empowerment for the impossible, reminiscent of the grace that was upon the apostles (Acts 4:33). This Great Grace brings a fresh excitement and a new level of acceleration in our walk with the Lord. It's a power that enables believers to witness the resurrection of Jesus Christ with great power.

This grace was first hinted at in the Old Testament, with the angel of the Lord referring to "grace, grace" in the context of Zerubbabel's commission to rebuild the temple (Zechariah 4:7). This same great grace is needed today for the spiritual rebuilding of the Church, preparing it for the return of our soon-coming King.

Our Father desires to release blessings, opportunities, and resources to us. This Great Grace will usher in an era of multiplication, as seen in the early Church where the disciples' dedication to the Word and prayer led to a rapid increase in their numbers (Acts 6:7). The key to accessing this grace is the anointing of the Holy Spirit. It's not by human might or power, but by God's Spirit that we will see the fulfillment of our destinies and the provision for our visions (Zechariah 4:6).

As we embrace this season, let us focus on intimacy with God. It is this intimacy that releases the power of God, which in turn releases favor. Favor comes through the anointing, which then releases the provision of God. In essence, favor, power, and provision are intertwined, each flowing from our relationship with God.

Let us move forward in faith, trusting in the anointing and the presence of God. As we do, we will see the supernatural provision of God manifest in our lives. It's a time to receive the anointing of great grace, to extend God's kingdom on earth. Let's open our hearts to this grace and believe together for a mighty move of God in our lives and ministries.

ABOUT THE AUTHOR

Diving deep into the realms of spiritual awakening, Bill Vincent embodies a connection with the Supernatural that spans over three decades. With a robust prophetic anointing, he has dedicated his life to ministry, serving as a guiding light and a pillar of strength in Revival Waves of Glory Ministries.

Bill Vincent is not just a Minister but a prolific Author, contributing to the spiritual enlightenment of many through his diverse range of writings and teachings. His work encompasses themes of deliverance, fostering the presence of God, and shaping Apostolic, cutting-edge Church structure. His insights are drawn from a wellspring of experience, steeped in Revival, and fine-tuned by a profound Spiritual Sensitivity.

In his relentless pursuit of God's Presence and his commitment to sustaining Revival, Bill focuses primarily on inviting divine encounters and maintaining a spiritual atmosphere ripe for transformation. His extensive library of over 125 books serves as a beacon of hope, guiding countless individuals in overcoming the shackles of Satan and embracing the light of God.

Revival Waves of Glory Ministries is not your typical church – it's a prophetic ministry, a sanctuary where the Holy Spirit is given the freedom to move as He wills. Our sermons, a blend of divine wisdom and revelation, can be experienced on Rumble, immersing you in the transformative power of the Word: https://rumble.com/c/revivalwavesofgloryministriesbillvincent

For a deeper exploration into our teachings, visions, and the manifold grace of God, visit https://www.revivalwavesofgloryministries.com/.

Embark on a journey of spiritual discovery with Bill Vincent, and let the waves of revival wash over you, unveiling the divine power and boundless love of God!

Podcast: https://podcasters.spotify.com/pod/show/billvincent2

Rumble: https://rumble.com/c/revivalwavesofgloryministriesbillvincent

Be sure to check out our new videos **Downloads From Heaven!**